W9-BVM-770

RATTLESNAKES

by Josh Gregory

Children's Press®

An Imprint of Scholastic Inc.

New York   Toronto   London   Auckland   Sydney
Mexico City   New Delhi   Hong Kong
Danbury, Connecticut

Content Consultant
Dr. Stephen S. Ditchkoff
Professor of Wildlife Sciences
Auburn University
Auburn, Alabama

Photographs ©: age fotostock/Norma Jean Gargasz: 38, 39; Alamy Images:
22, 23 (Bill Gorum), 10, 11 (Danita Delimont), 2 main, 3 main, 24 (Photoshot
Holdings Ltd), 31 (Robert E. Barber), 8, 9 (Robert Hamilton), 34, 35 (Wayne
Hughes); Animals Animals: 5 bottom, 40, 41 (Berquist, Paul & Joyce), 28
(Leszczynski, Zigmund); Dreamstime: 1, 46 (Isselee), 2 background, 3
background, 44, 45 (Piotr Gilko); Getty Images: 36 (Bloomberg), 27 (Marc
Crumpler), 12 (PHOTO 24); iStockphoto/michaklootwijk: 4, 5 background, 32,
33; Minden Pictures/James Christensen: cover; Science Source/E. R. Degginger:
18, 19; Shutterstock, Inc.: 6, 7 (Heiko Kiera), 20, 21 (visuelldesign); Superstock,
Inc.: 14, 15 (age fotostock), 5 top, 16 (Wayne Lynch/All Canada Photos).

Map by Bob Italiano

Library of Congress Cataloging-in-Publication Data
Gregory, Josh, author.
  Rattlesnakes / by Josh Gregory.
    pages cm. — (Nature's children)
  Summary: "This book details the life and habits of rattlesnakes."—
Provided by publisher.
  Audience: Ages 9–12.
  Audience: Grades 4 to 6.
  ISBN 978-0-531-21167-0 (library binding)
  ISBN 978-0-531-21186-1 (pbk.)
1. Rattlesnakes–Juvenile literature. I.
Title. II. Series: Nature's children
(New York, N.Y.)
  QL666.O69G74 2015
  597.96'38—dc23
                       2014029893

Printed in China 62
SCHOLASTIC, CHILDREN'S PRESS, and associated logos are
trademarks and/or registered trademarks of Scholastic Inc.

1 2 3 4 5 6 7 8 9 10 R 24 23 22 21 20 19 18 17 16 15

Rattlesnakes

Class	Reptilia
Order	Squamata
Family	Viperidae
Genera	2 genera (*Crotalus* and *Sistrurus*)
Species	Around 30 species
World distribution	North, Central, and South America, ranging from southern Canada to central Argentina
Habitats	Deserts, grasslands, wetlands
Distinctive physical characteristics	Most species range from 2 to 4 feet (0.6 to 1.2 meters) in length; keratin rattle at tip of tail; forked tongue; pointed, venomous fangs; long, muscular bodies; different species display wide range of colors and patterns
Habits	Most species rest during the day and hunt at night; adults eat infrequently and often consume large amounts of food at once; species in temperate climates hibernate in the winter; females reproduce about once every two years and breed during the spring
Diet	All species are carnivorous; exact diet depends on size and habitat of the snake; rodents and birds are especially common prey

RATTLESNAKES

Contents

CHAPTER 1

Snakes in the Grass

A group of hikers enjoy the sunny afternoon as they make their way along a trail in the southwestern United States. The sights from the desert path are breathtaking. Rock formations tower in the distance, and wild grasses sway gently in the breeze. The hikers know that they have more to look out for than just beautiful landforms and plant life, though.

As the hiker in the lead turns along a bend in the trail, she sees a snake lying along the path, basking in the warmth of the sun. The snake notices the hiker right away. The tip of its tail begins to shake rapidly, producing a rattling noise. It's a western diamondback rattlesnake! The hiker warns her friends to stay put and backs away slowly as the snake speeds off in the other direction. With the danger past, the hikers and the snake are both able to enjoy the sunshine in peace.

A western diamondback uses its rattling tail to scare off people and other potential threats.

Sizing Up Snakes

Like all snakes, rattlesnakes have long, muscular bodies with a head at one end and a tail at the other. They lack legs and arms and are covered in scales. Different colored scales are arranged to form patterns such as stripes or diamonds on the snake's body. These colors and patterns vary widely from species to species.

The smallest rattlesnake species is the pigmy rattlesnake, which reaches a maximum length of around 1 foot (30.5 centimeters). The largest is the eastern diamondback, which can measure up to 8 feet (2.4 meters) long. Most other species grow to be between 2 and 4 feet (0.6 to 1.2 m) long.

Adult male
6 ft. (1.8 m)

Smallest rattlesnake
1 ft. (30.5 cm) long

Largest rattlesnake
8 ft. (2.4 m) long

Dusky pigmy rattlesnakes live across the southeastern United States.

Remarkable Rattles

The feature that sets a rattlesnake apart from other kinds of snakes is the rattle at the tip of its tail. All but one rattlesnake species have this remarkable noisemaker. A rattle is made out of keratin, which is the same substance that makes up human fingernails. Several rings of this hard material fit together to form the rattle.

The snake can shake its tail very quickly. In fact, the muscles in a rattlesnake's tail are among the fastest known to exist in any animal. They can vibrate back and forth more than 50 times per second. When a snake shakes its tail, the rings of keratin bounce against each other. This creates the snake's distinctive rattling sound. Rattlesnakes use this noise to warn potential predators and other large animals to stay away. This keeps the snake from being bothered and protects the other animals from being bit.

Wild rattlesnakes rarely have more than 10 segments in their rattles, and segments often break off of the end.

All Over America

Rattlesnakes occupy a fairly wide range. They can be found in many places throughout North, Central, and South America. Wild rattlesnakes live as far north as southern Canada and reach all the way south to central Argentina. However, they are most commonly found in northern Mexico and the southwestern United States.

Because they have such a large range, rattlesnakes can be found in many different habitats. Deserts are home to the widest variety of rattlesnake species. These species feel right at home in hot, dry climates. Some species prefer the warm, wet swamps of the southeastern United States, while others thrive in grassy meadows or forests. Some live high up in mountainous regions, while others live at low elevations. Each species is suited to its native environment and has specific needs for weather conditions, shelter, and available prey.

Many rattlesnakes are comfortable swimming through water.

CHAPTER 2

Serpent Strengths

Rattlesnakes are fearsome hunters. All species are carnivores. They prey upon a variety of smaller animals. Rodents such as mice, chipmunks, rats, and squirrels make up a large part of many rattlesnakes' diets. Rabbits, lizards, birds, and toads are also common food items. Some rattlesnakes even eat smaller kinds of snakes. Diets vary from species to species, depending on how large the rattlesnake is and what prey animals are available in its habitat.

Even though they are skilled predators, most rattlesnakes do not spend much time searching for food. They only hunt when they are hungry, and a single meal might keep an adult rattlesnake satisfied for around two weeks. The larger the meal, the longer the snake can go before it needs to eat again. Young rattlesnakes eat more often than older ones because they need more nutrients to keep growing.

A timber rattlesnake widens its mouth to swallow a red squirrel.

A Snake's Senses

Rattlesnakes have sharp senses to help them locate prey. Due to their small eyes and lack of external ears, they do not have very good eyesight or hearing. However, they make up for these weaknesses with other unique senses.

Every rattlesnake has two special sense organs called pits. The pits are located on either side of the snake's head, between its eyes and nostrils. They are very sensitive to the heat given off by prey animals' bodies. A rattlesnake can use this sense to accurately find prey even when it is completely dark outside.

As rattlesnakes move around, they constantly flick their long, forked tongues in and out of their mouths. The tongue picks up scents from the ground and the air. These scents are processed in a special organ called the Jacobson's organ. It is located inside the snake's snout, with two openings in the mouth. The snake searches for and follows certain scents to find prey.

A rattlesnake flicks its tongue out to sample the scents in its surroundings.

Fearsome Fangs

Many of the animals that rattlesnakes eat are fast runners. However, rattlesnakes do not hunt by chasing down this speedy prey. Instead, the snakes find a place to hide and wait for opportunities to **ambush** their targets. When the prey comes near, the snake suddenly springs forward. Its mouth is wide open, and its extremely sharp fangs point forward. As the snake bites into the unlucky animal, it injects **venom** through its fangs.

The venom is produced in **glands** in the snake's head. When the snake bites, it decides how much venom to use. Larger prey might require more venom. Different rattlesnake species produce different kinds of venom, but with the same results. Once bitten, the prey is poisoned and begins to die. The snake follows its target and waits until the prey is no longer able to move. Then the snake opens its mouth and swallows its meal whole.

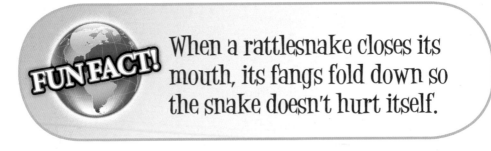

FUN FACT! When a rattlesnake closes its mouth, its fangs fold down so the snake doesn't hurt itself.

A timber rattlesnake opens its mouth wide as it lunges out to strike prey.

Dangers and Defenses

Even though rattlesnakes are dangerous, they still face threats from other powerful hunters. Coyotes, foxes, bobcats, and a number of bird species all feed on rattlesnakes. Another common predator is the king snake. These large snakes lack venom of their own, but they are **immune** to the poisonous bites of rattlesnakes. Younger, smaller rattlesnakes are especially vulnerable to attacks from predators.

While rattlesnakes can use their fangs to defend themselves against most predators, they prefer to avoid a fight whenever possible. One way they do this is by using their natural **camouflage** to stay hidden. The colors and patterns of each species' scales help it blend in with its surroundings. Because snakes spend so much time lying still, it can be difficult for predators to spot them. If an animal gets too close, a snake rattles its tail and makes hissing sounds with its mouth. It might also puff up its body to make itself look larger than it actually is.

This western diamondback rattlesnake's yellow-orange coloring blends in well with its surroundings.

Warm in the Winter

Like all **reptiles**, rattlesnakes are cold-blooded. This means that their body temperatures rise and fall depending on how warm or cold the air is around them. They cannot survive in extreme temperatures. To help regulate their body temperatures, rattlesnakes can often be found lying in the sunlight to warm up or hiding in the shade to cool down.

Most rattlesnakes live in habitats where the weather is fairly warm all year long. However, some live in places where they have to deal with long periods of cold weather during the winter. In order to keep from freezing to death, some rattlesnake species **hibernate** during the coldest months of the year. They crawl into underground **dens** and pile together with hundreds of other snakes. Many different snake species hibernate in the same den. Together, they sleep through the winter and emerge in spring.

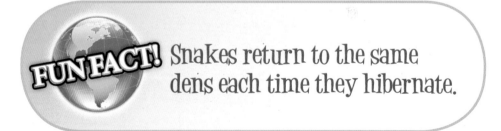

FUN FACT! Snakes return to the same dens each time they hibernate.

Northern black-tailed and western diamondback rattlesnakes hole up together in a den to hibernate.

CHAPTER 3

A Snake's Life

Rattlesnakes lead mostly **solitary** lives. They are not **territorial**, but they also do not seek out company or communicate often with other snakes. They simply keep to themselves and try to avoid other animals during most times of the year.

Most of a rattlesnake's time is spent hiding and resting. Rattlesnakes are mostly inactive during the day. They find a comfortable, hidden spot where the temperature is just right and wait for the sun to go down. If a snake is hungry, it might spend the night looking for prey. Because it relies mainly on its Jacobson's organ and pits to find its way around, the darkness does not matter. If the snake has eaten recently, it might simply spend the night continuing to rest.

A rattlesnake is most likely to look for food at night.

Meeting a Mate

Aside from the months they spend hibernating in dens, the only time rattlesnakes seek out the company of other snakes is during mating season. All rattlesnakes mate in the spring. During this time, males compete for the attention of females. One way they do this is through a process called combat dancing. During a combat dance, two males raise the front portions of their bodies, wrap around each other, and try to wrestle each other to the ground. Eventually, one of the snakes gives up and slithers away. The winner is left to mate with a nearby female. Neither snake is injured during the combat dance.

While male rattlesnakes mate every year, a female usually mates every other year. Around 90 days after mating, the female is ready to give birth. Most snakes lay eggs that hatch after the mother has left them behind. However, rattlesnakes are ovoviviparous. This means a rattlesnake mother carries her babies in soft eggs inside her body until they are ready to be born.

Two rattlesnakes face off in a graceful combat dance.

Starting Out Small

Most rattlesnake species give birth to between four and 10 babies at a time. However, some species might produce as many as 60 offspring in a single **brood**. When a baby rattlesnake is first born, it is wrapped in a thin, clear sac. It pokes its head through the wrapping and slithers out. Rattlesnake mothers do not protect their babies or help them find food. Instead, the newborn snakes must fend for themselves.

Newborn rattlesnakes look almost exactly like smaller versions of their parents. They have working fangs and can produce venom as soon as they are born. However, they do not yet have fully developed rattles. Instead, their tails are tipped with a single layer of keratin called a button. As snakes grow, they shed their skin. Each time a rattlesnake sheds, a new layer of keratin is added to its rattle. A baby rattlesnake first sheds when it is around one or two weeks old.

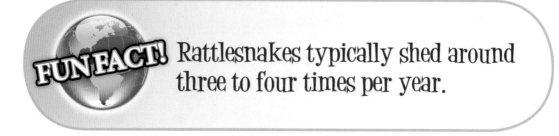

FUN FACT! Rattlesnakes typically shed around three to four times per year.

This newborn timber rattlesnake has the same markings as its mother.

CHAPTER 4

Ancient Animals

The earliest ancestors of snakes lived more than 100 million years ago. Unlike modern snakes, these ancient animals were probably lizards that walked around on legs. Over time, they developed into limbless animals that closely resemble modern snakes. The earliest known fossil of a modern snake dates back roughly 65 million to 70 million years.

Today, there are thousands of snake species living all around the world. About 30 of those snake species are classified as rattlesnakes. These species are organized into two genera. Most rattlesnakes belong to the genus *Crotalus*. These species are sometimes called true rattlesnakes. Other rattlesnakes belong to the *Sistrurus* genus. They are smaller than their *Crotalus* cousins. *Sistrurus* can also be identified by the nine large scales on the tops of their heads.

Fossils of snakes that lived millions of years ago have been discovered around the world.

Specialized Species

Some rattlesnake species have unique abilities and physical features that make them stand out from their relatives. For example, rattlesnake species typically move headfirst. But the North American sidewinder is the only one that moves using an S-shaped sideways motion. This helps these snakes move quickly along the sandy surfaces of their desert habitat.

The only rattlesnake species that doesn't have a working rattle is the Santa Catalina Island rattlesnake. Even as adults, these snakes continue to have only a button at the tip of their tail. Unlike other rattlesnakes, this snake doesn't add a layer of keratin to its tail when it sheds. Instead, its button falls off and is replaced each time. The lack of a rattle actually helps these snakes. They hunt by climbing up into trees or bushes and snatching mice, lizards, and birds. A working rattle would create too much noise for the snakes to take their prey by surprise.

A sidewinder leaves unusual tracks in the sand as it moves.

A Rattlesnake's Relatives

Rattlesnakes belong to a larger group of snakes called vipers. There are more than 200 different viper species. They are grouped together based on their fangs. All of these snakes have the same kind of pointed, venomous fangs that rattlesnakes use to subdue their prey. They live throughout many parts of the world in a wide range of habitats and can vary greatly in appearance and behavior.

The largest viper is the bushmaster, which can grow up to 10 feet (3 m) long. This massive predator hunts even less frequently than a rattlesnake. It might eat fewer than 10 times a year, staying still for weeks at a time as it waits for prey to pass by.

The water moccasin is found in the swamps of the southeastern United States. This deadly viper is sometimes called the cottonmouth, due to the white coloring on the inside of its mouth. It is a strong swimmer, and it often hunts prey such as fish and frogs.

Other vipers include jumping vipers, which can leap into the air as they strike.

Cottonmouths spend a lot of their time in or near water.

CHAPTER 5

Relationships with Rattlesnakes

Throughout history, humans and snakes have had a complicated relationship. Many ancient peoples believed that snakes had mystical powers. Today, many people still find rattlesnakes to be mysterious animals. Because of their unusual appearance and venomous fangs, people are often afraid of them. This fear has led to people killing rattlesnakes. Some state governments have even paid **bounties** to people who could prove that they killed rattlesnakes in certain areas. Rattlesnakes are sometimes hunted for other reasons as well. Rattlesnake skin is valuable. It can be used to make boots, handbags, and many other decorative and clothing items. Some people also eat rattlesnake meat.

Partially because of such hunting, populations of some rattlesnake species have shrunk greatly in recent decades. They have even become **endangered** in areas where they once thrived.

Some people collect rattlesnake venom to use in antivenom treatments for snakebites and in scientific research.

Staying Safe

The safest way to deal with rattlesnakes is to stay as far away from them as you can. However, if you spend time in an area where these snakes are common, you might accidentally come across one. If you spot a snake, never try to approach it. Instead, give the snake plenty of room to escape. Back away slowly. The snake will likely slither off to find a new hiding place. Remember that rattlesnakes would always prefer not to fight.

Rattlesnake bites can cause serious injury or even death in humans if they are left untreated. If you or someone you know is bit, you should go to a hospital as quickly as possible. With proper treatment, most snakebites do not cause serious problems. In the United States, poisonous snakes bite around 8,000 people every year. Only a small handful of these people die.

A hiker should always be aware of his or her surroundings.

Here to Stay

Even though they may seem strange or frightening, rattlesnakes deserve care and respect. Like all plants and animals, they play an important role in keeping their ecosystems balanced. As predators, they help keep populations of animals such as rats and mice from growing too large. In turn, this keeps the rattlesnakes' prey from eating too many plants.

In order to keep this balance in place, we must avoid harming rattlesnakes. Conservation groups work to protect rattlesnakes. Some also work to increase the population of species that have been affected by overhunting and other human activities. They breed the snakes in safe places, such as zoos, and then introduce them back into wild habitats. These groups also work to educate people about the proper way to deal with snakes. With enough hard work, more people will learn the truth about these astonishing animals, and rattlesnakes will have a long, healthy future ahead of them.

Biologist Matt Goode takes a look at a tiger rattlesnake found in the wild.

Words to Know

ambush (AM-bush) — to attack from a hiding place

ancestors (AN-ses-turz) — ancient animal species that are related to modern species

bounties (BOUN-teez) — rewards offered for the capture of a criminal or harmful animal

brood (BROOD) — a group of young snakes who all hatched at the same time

camouflage (KAM-o-flaj) — coloring or body shape that allows an animal to blend in with its surroundings

carnivores (KAHR-nuh-vorz) — animals that eat meat

climates (KLYE-mits) — the weather typical of places over long periods of time

conservation (kon-sur-VAY-shun) — the act of protecting an environment and the things that live in it

dens (DENZ) — the homes of wild animals

ecosystems (EE-koh-sis-tuhmz) — communities that include all the living things in a place and their relation to the environment

elevations (el-uh-VAY-shuhnz) — heights above sea level

endangered (en-DAYN-jurd) — at risk of becoming extinct, usually because of human activity

fossil (FAH-suhl) — a bone, shell, or other trace of an animal or plant from millions of years ago, preserved as rock

genera (JEN-ur-uh) — groups of related plants or animals that are larger than a species but smaller than a family glands (GLANDZ) — organs in the body that produce or release natural chemicals

habitats (HAB-uh-tats) — places where an animal or a plant is usually found

hibernate (HYE-bur-nate) — to sleep through the winter in order to survive when temperatures are cold and food is hard to find

immune (i-MYOON) — not influenced or affected by something

mating (MAYT-ing) — joining together to produce babies

ovoviviparous (oh-voh-vye-VIH-puh-russ) — producing eggs that develop within the maternal body (as of various fishes or reptiles) and hatch within or immediately after release from the parent

predators (PREH-duh-turz) — animals that live by hunting other animals for food

prey (PRAY) — an animal that's hunted by another animal for food

range (RAYNJ) — the overall area where an animal can be found

reptiles (REP-tylz) — cold-blooded animals that crawl across the ground or creep on short legs; most reptiles have backbones and reproduce by laying eggs

scales (SKAYLZ) — thin, flat, overlapping pieces of hard skin that cover the body of a fish, snake, or certain other animals

solitary (SOL-ih-tehr-ee) — preferring to live alone

species (SPEE-sheez) — one of the groups into which animals and plants of the same genus are divided; members of the same species can mate and have offspring

territorial (terr-uh-TOR-ee-uhl) — defensive of a certain area

venom (VEH-num) — poison produced by some animals

Habitat Map

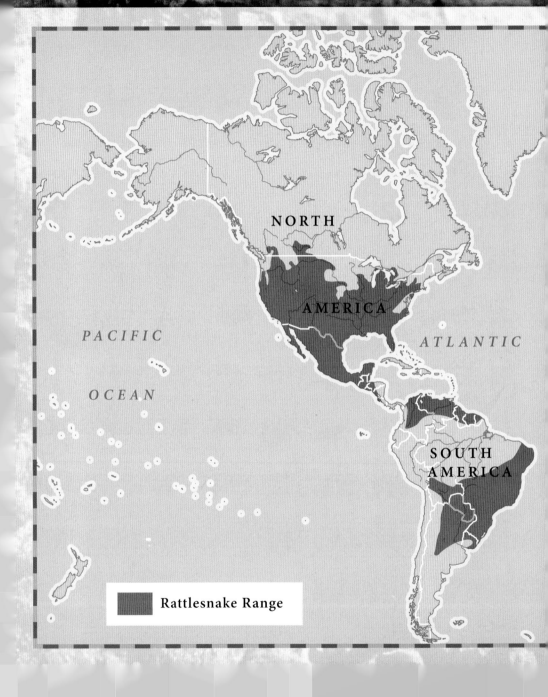

NORTH

AMERICA

PACIFIC

OCEAN

ATLANTIC

SOUTH
AMERICA

Rattlesnake Range

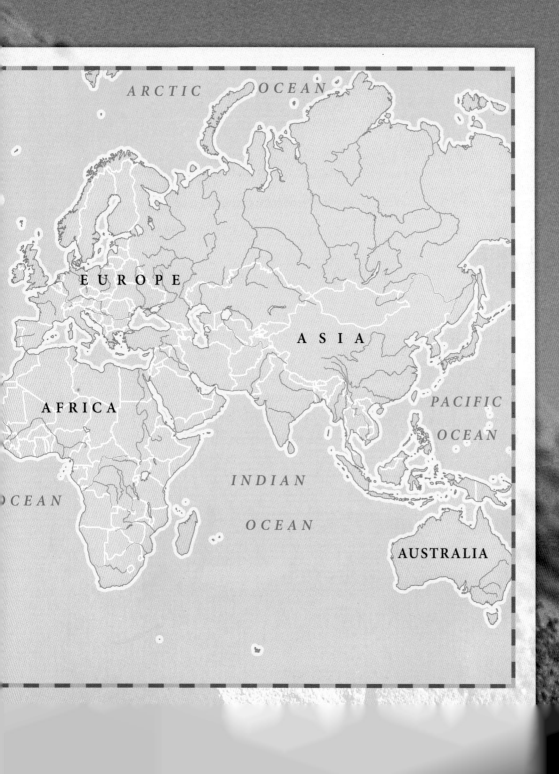

Find Out More

Books

Leigh, Autumn. *Diamondback Rattlesnake*. New York: Gareth Stevens Publishing, 2011.

Stewart, Melissa. *Snakes!* Washington, DC: National Geographic, 2009.

Woodward, John. *Everything You Need to Know About Snakes*. New York: DK Publishing, 2013.

Visit this Scholastic Web site for more information on rattlesnakes:
www.factsfornow.scholastic.com
Enter the keyword **Rattlesnakes**

Index

Page numbers in *italics* indicate a photograph or map.

About the Author

Josh Gregory writes and edits books for kids. He lives in Chicago, Illinois.